RETIREMENT?
It's More Than Dollars

By Les Hoffman

© Copyright 2020

I0505520

INTRODUCTION

Imagine, just for a moment, that you already have all the money you need to retire. You have reached the point of financial independence from your job. Let's assume you can keep working if you want to; the decision is entirely up to you.

Feels pretty good, doesn't it?

Now, I'm going to throw a couple of questions at you:

Would you say that your job provides much of your purpose for living, or is it more a means to an end?

Without your job, do you think you would lose a big part of your self-image and identity?

For most people, these are tough questions that take some deliberation.

Okay...given it some thought?

"Yes" answers to these questions imply a strong emotional link to your job. With this connection, walking away from employment and replacing it with new activities is a scary proposition.

And why should you? Perhaps you feel fully satisfied and self-fulfilled with your working lifestyle. If this sounds like you, retiring from your job is probably not the right decision to make.

But maybe you're someone who doesn't find a typical workday all that fulfilling. Sure, it has its moments, but perhaps too often you find yourself just talking on the phone, sitting in meetings, or staring at a computer screen. Maybe you yearn for something else—a chance to live life on your own terms without the daily dictates of a job. A chance to try new things, re-discover old passions and discover new ones. If this sounds more like you, then retirement may be just what you're looking for. About 10,000 Americans retire every day.

These descriptions represent the basic motivations of people at both ends of the retirement conundrum. Both positions are understandable and deserve respect. Disparaging remarks about either position (e.g., a "workaholic" employee or a "lazy" retiree) show a lack of understanding and maturity.

Most people find themselves somewhere in between. They may have to retire by a certain age, or they may have a choice of when (or if) they will retire. They've worked most of their lives and might be ready for a change, but they don't really know anything else. They think about their family, past vacations, and what they currently like to do in their free time. They try to envision a life built around these things, but wonder if that vision is really feasible. They're intrigued by the opportunities of retirement, but when it comes down to it, they're not sure what they would do on a day-to-day basis without a job. Their difficulty is that they fully understand working life but have not had the opportunity to try out retired life. They wonder: Maybe better the devil they know? They are understandably scared of the unknowns of retirement and the seeming finality of that decision.

This book shows what it takes to thrive as a retiree, and it answers the questions that come up when contemplating entry into this new phase of life.

When deciding whether or not to do something, it's often instructive to hear from people who have faced the same decision, made their choice, and experienced the result. You'll hear from several recent and long-time retirees, including one who has since gone back to work.

Building wealth is the necessary first step toward a successful retirement, and this book provides a sound investment strategy that will work at any career stage. But money only provides the means, not the emotional fuel and initiative needed for a fulfilling experience. Retirees that ignore these needs have difficulty guiding their daily activities.

In these pages, you'll find an honest discussion

about the emotional and psychological side of retirement. All the money in the world can't buy a fulfilling retirement experience without the right attitude, preparation, and commitment. Inside this book is a proven guide to a successful retirement; not just in dollars, but in mind, body, and spirit.

No matter how you currently feel about retirement, I hope you read these pages with an open mind and a sense of adventure. To keep things fun, I have added a short, thought-provoking note at the end of each section, based on my observations over the years. I hope a few of these "Words of Wisdom" (*W.O.W.*) resonate with your personal life.

So let's get started and try to answer the question: RETIRE?

W.O.W.

Never sell a used car to a friend.

TABLE OF CONTENTS

CHAPTER 1
RETIREMENT CONCEPTS

CHAPTER 1

RETIREMENT CONCEPTS

What is Retirement?

I think most people would agree that the definition of retirement includes the cessation of work as a necessary means to fund the basic requirements of life. Many would add to this by saying a basic characteristic of retirement is the absence of work activities dictated by others. In other words, a retired person is someone that is financially independent and only performs work that they want to do, under their own direction. It's a personal freedom from the occupational demands of others.

We all love personal freedom; however, freedom comes with responsibility--the responsibility to guide our own activities. We can't avoid this even if we wanted to. The choice to do nothing is still a choice, and a retired person makes their own choices and lives with the results.

I remember just before I retired, someone asked me

what I was going to do all day. Depending on how it's asked, this can be a legitimate question, but the tone from this individual was obviously derogatory; this person was not really interested in what I was planning to do each day in retirement. He had already made up his mind that retirement is a bad idea. Translated: "You're stupid. You haven't thought this through and are making a big mistake." I had come to recognize this attitude, and responded back: "I'm going to get drunk every day and watch Beverly Hillbillies reruns on TV".

Conversation over, argument avoided.

The point of this story is that when you quit your job, you don't retire from life, you retire from work and the life centered around it. Retirement is a new beginning—a new life. You should retire to do something you enjoy, not just to stop doing something. It's a time for self-growth and discovery. It's a time to do what you couldn't do while you were still working.

A few years after I left work, my son told me I had "re-invented" myself. Although this term may be a little drastic, there's some truth there. I didn't so much change as a person (although I do eat a lot slower now!), but rather I applied myself to a number of new (and old) things in a way I could never have done if I had still been employed.

In Chapter 3, we will discuss how to develop a list of potential retirement activities tailored to your interests. Many of these interests will have their roots in childhood and young adulthood. When you work, you tend to forget things you cared so much about when you were younger, and instead devote yourself to necessary and practical matters, including, for many of us, raising children. When retirement nears, you should remind yourself of these past interests and get back in touch with your former enthusiasms. Armed with maturity, knowledge, and time, you can often find an enjoyable outlet for some of your original passions.

This touches on an unavoidable paradox of the retirement decision. The longer you work, the less you know how to fill your days on your own in a fulfilling manner, and the less time you have before making your retirement decision. To escape this paradox requires a conscious effort while you are still employed.

Retirement should be viewed as one of life's phases. If you are planning to retire, learn to look forward to it with a spirit of adventure and a sense of humor. If you feel forced to do it, or are fearful of it, those negative feelings can manifest themselves as a self-fulfilling prophecy.

Most successfully retired people enjoy the daily pleasures of life, the satisfaction of reaching their potential in one or more areas, and the spiritual peace that results from living their dream and growing as a person.

The retirement discussed in this book isn't centered around reflecting on life and preparing to die. We may or may not ever get to that point someday, but this book isn't about that. It's about building a new life of your own making while you still have the health, enthusiasm, and dollars to make it happen.

W.O.W.

The power of belief is the greatest power.

Is This Something I Want?

Simple question, right?

Not really.

The difficulty is that you can't try it out first, before committing. Later, we will discuss strategies to help mitigate this situation. But there's no escaping the basic truth that without actually retiring, you are left with your imagination and intuition as to what it will really be like for you.

What are the things that you might give up when you decide to quit your job and retire? How important are these things to you? Will your "new life" in retirement more than compensate for their loss?

Perhaps even harder to answer right now: Are you emotionally ready for retirement?

Let's try and answer these questions together, or at

least make you aware of the things you should consider before making your retirement decision.

W.O.W.

Creative Thinking is Limited by Vocabulary

Tangible Trade-offs

Big decisions always involve trade-offs. When you decide between two courses of action, you give up something to get something else.

The fundamental trade-off in a retirement decision is time versus money. When you retire, you give up income in exchange for free time. Maybe you already have a pretty good idea of how you plan to spend your time in retirement. If not, the suggestions in Chapter 3 can help you get started. Assuming you can afford to retire, can the extra income you would earn through continued work buy things that are more important to you than the free time to pursue your plans for retirement? If you aren't sure, you should try out your ideas for retirement activities while you're still working. If you can't find the time to do this under your current work schedule, consider switching to a part-time arrangement that will provide extra time without giving up all the extra income.

Time away from work is a limited and necessary

commodity. We all need time to take our car to the shop, go to the doctor, and handle emergencies. But time away from work can also be precious if it helps us expand our minds and improve our social relationships. Let's face it--some jobs, especially office jobs, feel unnatural to many workers. For these people, sitting at a desk during waking hours, day after day, is tedious and something to endure, not enjoy. Retirement provides these people with an opportunity to change their lives for the better.

There are some people who feel a duty to work as long as possible in order to bequeath large sums of money to their children. Extra income beyond their own needs is gifted, put in trust, or provided in the form of an inheritance. Postponing retirement for this purpose is well-intended, but should be carefully considered. Children often have difficulty growing up strong and independent if they are given or promised substantial sums of money. The irony here is that most giving seniors are self-made individuals who didn't have their wealth provided to them by rich relations. Having to make their own way amid the trials of life made them the successful people they are, just as it would their children.

Perhaps you share another common concern about retirement--the loss of daily contact with co-workers. Besides the inherent social value, many may be your friends. But leaving work doesn't mean leaving these friendships behind. They are still your friends, and you can see them away from work, at lunch, and maybe even an occasional office visit. You will also make new friends in your retirement activities and have the time to travel and see out-of-town friends. The reality here is that you will likely expand your social network, not shrink it. Even better, many of the new friends you make will share your passions, since they will be participants in your chosen activities.

What about weekends, holidays, and vacation? Some people say "I've always loved weekends and vacations during my working career. I don't want to lose that excitement." Let's put this notion to rest right now. Weekends and vacations are still exciting in retirement. Remember that retirement is a new life filled with activities and a new structure that you enjoy and have chosen yourself. You will still enjoy kicking back, relaxing, traveling, and doing things that are not part of your daily routine. The difference is you don't do it to escape, and you don't worry so much about catching up once it's over.

You might read this trade-off discussion and say "Sounds good, but this guy's trying to paint a rosy picture for me. I'm worried the reality will be sitting at home on the couch with nothing to do and no one to talk to. I'll no longer be engaged in the "real" world anymore."

Can this depressing scenario really happen to somebody? Of course it can.

Like anything else, you get out of retirement what you put into it. A successful retirement takes planning, initiative, and a good attitude. Without these, nothing I say will make retirement a great experience for you. Somebody once said "Retirement's not for sissies". They were right.

You have to ask yourself: "Does the potential of this "new life" in retirement--the adventure, exploration, personal growth and activities of my own choosing excite me? Am I willing to take the initiative and fully leverage this newfound freedom?" If you can answer yes to these questions, then keep reading. The rewards can be tremendous.

W.O.W.

In business, try to look at something one time and then take action. It's inefficient to review something, put it down, then review it again later.

Emotional Considerations

Retirement provides fundamental, life-changing opportunities. A chance to savor your working achievements while starting a new life centered around family, friends, and your own passions.

But are you ready for it? Not just financially, but emotionally?

Besides a paycheck and a schedule of daily activities, there are other losses caused by retirement. These losses are psychological in nature and go to the heart of the retirement dilemma for some financially-independent workers. Their jobs are such an integral part of their lives and identity that they are understandably fearful of retirement.

Someone preparing for a successful retirement should have a balanced home life and work life. Their basic personality and self-image, their persona, is not tied to one or the other and is constant regardless of their environment. They know who they are and carry this confidence wherever they go.

Why is this important? Let's go through some of the positive emotional perks that arise from a successful career, and I want you to ask yourself how much you'll miss them. Please be honest with yourself, because all of these factors have a certain allure, and tend to reinforce a positive self-image. It takes a healthy measure of self-confidence to give them up in retirement.

We've already talked about the tangible loss of a paycheck (money). But how about the emotional loss? Cash and the things it can buy are especially prized in our consumer culture. We're inundated with advertising trying to equate success with the ownership of things. There are plenty of people who believe in this and live their lives accordingly. For these people, the difference in driving a Honda, instead of a Mercedes, is profound. These people often judge others more on what they own than on who they really are. Some of them may look at you differently if you decide to downsize a bit in retirement. Will their approval be greatly missed?

Regarding income, some of you may be in a "Golden Handcuffs" situation. "Golden Handcuffs" is a term coined in the 70's that refers to employees that are so highly compensated (income and benefits) that they can't bring themselves to leave their job, even if they don't really need the money to live comfortably. This is more a psychological/emotional dilemma than a financial issue.

Understandably, after years of work finally result in the attainment of a highly compensated position, it just feels wrong to leave, even if the income and benefits are no longer required. Typically, this fades quickly into the rearview mirror after retirement.

I'm going to assume that if you are financially capable of retiring, you have had a fairly successful career. Maybe you've reached a position of relative power and authority within your business; i.e., people listen to you, maybe they work for you. You have probably earned a measure of respect within the workplace, a certain status or prestige. To some extent, this will change in retirement. You will likely be on a more level playing field with your new peer group(s). This is not necessarily a bad thing, but it bears your consideration. Also, depending on where you now work, the people you will regularly see in retirement may not be as educated as your work-friends. Will you be able to enjoy the more frequent company of people with varying degrees of education and intellect?

One of the toughest things you lose in retirement is the sense of belonging you have in a workplace. Even a difficult job can form a strong sense of camaraderie. "We're all in this together" is a powerful bonding force. I'm not going to try and sugarcoat this negative factor. It's human nature to seek a sense of belonging in our lives. We are social creatures, after all. Of course, there are ample opportunities to join other groups in retirement, and most people belong to a strong family group. One of the main reasons people retire is to spend more time with their family. The point here is that you will likely feel the change in your workplace "membership". Can you become comfortable in a less frequent, more social relationship with your old work group?

Something else to consider: When we're working, we're used to being judged and graded. We strive to have that great performance review, that next promotion, that bonus check, or at least a heartfelt "attaboy". Basically, we like to "win" and to be recognized for it. This type of approval from others is not as readily available in retirement. Some retirement activities provide a form of this, but, in general, the work/reward system will not be replaced. In retirement, maintaining your successful identity and self-image will have to come more from within.

By achieving financial independence, you've made a great start.

Here's a tough one for you. Do you still feel a need to prove yourself in your career? If you retire, will you regret not having achieved more at your job? These are questions that only you can answer, but before retiring, you need to put to rest.

In that same regard, do you consider yourself indispensable at your place of employment? Will you be unable to relax in retirement, always feeling the need to check up on how your old business is performing and take action if it's not up to your standards? These are important questions in assessing your emotional readiness to retire. Once you leave work, unless you plan to stay on part-time or as a consultant, you owe it to the business to let the people on the job do their work. These people will probably do just fine, given a little time and independence. In most cases, the workplace can be thought of as a swimming pool. When you get out and leave, the hole you leave behind won't last very long.

Some people are scared to retire because they fear running out of money before they die. This can often be an irrational fear. Do your homework, run the numbers, and convince yourself that you have enough to retire (see Chapter 3). The mathematics don't lie. Of course, you can always conceive of a doomsday scenario where all your best-laid plans are destroyed, but in most of these scenarios you would be better off running for the hills with food, water and a gun versus trying to accumulate more money.

Lastly, and perhaps most importantly, you need to feel comfortable with yourself as a person before you take the leap to retirement. This doesn't mean that you don't have human problems. We all do. But it means that you understand your limitations and you trust yourself. You're not afraid to spend time by yourself; in fact, you are your own best friend and enjoy your own company.

The truth is that you will likely spend more time by yourself in retirement than you're used to. I'm not saying retirees are hermits (far from it), but you will likely no longer spend all your waking hours among a familiar group of people. In Chapter 3, we discuss putting together a list of your planned retirement activities. A few of those activities should be things that you enjoy on your own.

You may already be good at understanding yourself and your feelings. It's a good life skill to have and hone, and becomes even more important in retirement. Good or bad, a fulltime job is certainly a distraction and can keep a person from taking the time to learn about themselves. For some, work provides a means of escape from dealing with their feelings, if only temporarily.

Retirement activities are usually not as big a distraction as a fulltime job. To fully leverage retirement life, you should be skilled at understanding yourself and living with your feelings rather than trying to escape them. This is the only way to grow as a person and take full advantage of retirement life.

For some, this process of understanding and coming to terms with feelings comes naturally. For others, it takes a little work and practice to be honest with yourself and accepting of your feelings. For still others, talking it out with someone is needed. However you get there, the important thing is to do it. Only then will you be free to reach your full potential.

W.O.W.

To reach your full potential, you must first accept/support/trust yourself.

Retiree Interview #1

Dale Kohler

Austin, Texas

Dale and his wife Jan are both in their sixties and both recently retired.

What made you decide to retire?

"I really didn't want to outlive my usefulness at the job. We were fortunate to be in the position where our outstanding debt was paid off, I had a good pension plan through my employer, and our grandkids live right here in Austin."

Do you regret not working longer?

"NO!"

Was retirement difficult to adjust to?

"A little bit for me. Part of my job was being on-call 24/7, and it was a little difficult moving to a slower-paced lifestyle. I was given the opportunity to work half-time for a year before I retired, and this totally helped me integrate into the retired lifestyle with my wife. We had never spent all day, every day together except for short durations like vacations. You know, I figured that being together after retirement would take some adjustment. Working half-time allowed both of us to adjust to each other slowly."

What things do you regularly enjoy doing?

"Generally, being outside and enjoying the fresh air. Also, volunteering when possible, attending events like music and film festivals, going to movies, and going to lunch or happy hour with former co-workers."

What are some of the best things about being retired?

"Being available for whatever, whenever; like for family events (happy and sad) and grandkid baby-sitting. Also not having to deal with rush hour traffic! And no more dreaded Sunday night panic. Also being able to sleep in if I want to, although this did take about a 3--4 month adjustment period. I also like working on projects with no deadline from the outside. If I don't finish something, I have the next day or week to finish it."

What are some of the worst things about being re-tired?

"Losing contact with coworkers and forgetting their names, and realizing that your work can get along fine without you. Oh yeah—trying to remember what day of the week it is."

Can you offer any advice for people considering re-tirement?

"Make sure retirement is right for you. Don't do it just because you're 65 or because your spouse has retired. And make sure you are financially set or have a plan to get there. I would also say that un-less you hated your job or couldn't wait to leave for some reason, try to stay in touch with the people you used to work with. Through the years, you probably spent more time with them than your own family. One last thing—try to figure out how much of your identity is work-related, and how much of it is other-related. Before you retire, decide if you will be happy not having that work identity any longer."

CHAPTER 2

THE RETIREMENT EXPERIENCE

Case Study—My Personal Retirement Story

My retirement story started when I was a sopho-more in college. It wasn't that I thought about re-tirement back then, but rather I had to commit to a specific degree program or risk losing credits to-ward my degree. During high school, I thought I might enjoy being a veterinarian. I loved working with animals. As I became more knowledgeable about the practice, however, I decided that it wasn't really what I had in mind. This prompted me to take a hard look at career selection versus long-term in-come potential.

I had been working part-time since the 8th grade, and enjoyed having my own money. Rightly or wrongly, I viewed college education as an income generator first, and a passion second. I looked at degree programs that had the biggest potential in-come for the years invested, and from that list I con-sidered which ones I might like. I reasoned that if I ended up working in a field that I didn't like, I would quickly earn enough money to enable a switch into a more enjoyable, but lower-paying, degree/posi-tion, without a big change in lifestyle. So began my training for a thirty-year career as a Mechanical En-gineer/Engineering Executive.

As it turned out, I enjoyed being an engineer, par-ticularly after I advanced far enough to have some autonomy, authority, and personal business relationships. Later, I came to realize that the same is true for most career fields.

I respected and enjoyed working for my last and main (twenty-three year) employer, Southwest Research Institute. I had no desire to work anywhere else. My initial college idea of earning enough money to provide the option of switching into a more enjoyable, lower-paying field transformed into a goal of financial independence for our family. My wife was a CPA doing part-time accounting work at home while looking after our two kids. This new goal of financial independence opened up the future possibility of doing whatever we wanted, regardless of income. When we set this goal as a family, we had not decided to make any career changes or retire once it was reached. We simply wanted to have those options, and at the same time feel financially secure. And then a pleasant surprise happened--as we got closer and closer to meeting the goal, work became more enjoyable! Without the necessity of constant income, working became more a choice than a requirement, providing a sense of control and independence in the workplace.

Keeping our retirement options open, we purchased a vacation home at our favorite getaway, the South Texas beach. We spent most of our free time there and got a feel for what it would be like to live there fulltime. The beach house had a separate apartment that we rented out long-term to pay our ownership expenses. We made this purchase twelve years before our retirement decision.

Years later, as I moved up in rank at the Institute, future advancement became limited--the end result of a long career with narrowing possibilities for interesting new challenges.

Having reached our goal of financial independence, we began to consider the real possibility of "early" retirement (before age 65). We also thought about continuing work and, philanthropy aside, how we might use the extra money. A bigger house in a nicer neighborhood was what we came up with, but that wasn't a very strong motivator for us.

As a first step toward possible retirement, we decided to sell our permanent residence and rent a home closer to my job. If we retired, we planned to move into the beach house fulltime. At this time, our kids were off at grad school and the Division I managed was in great shape with excellent prospects. The conditions were right to retire. We proceeded to complete the necessary preparations for retirement (Chapter 3).

The last thing holding us back was the chance of one last promotion at the Institute. The position of interest was different than any I had held before and provided a real chance to influence the direction of the entire business. However, it was capably manned at the time, and after some discreet inquiries, I was able to determine that the position was not going to open up anytime in the foreseeable future.

So, we pulled the trigger.

I gave several months of notice and we made our final arrangements for an orderly retirement. I was 51 years old at the time, my wife 47.

The general reactions to my announcement were ones of support and shock. Several people were convinced there was more to the story; i.e., I would never have voluntarily stepped aside. Others worried I was making a mistake; my energy level was too high to move into their vision of retirement. One close friend came over to my house, unannounced, to inquire about my health. He was convinced I had some kind of terminal illness!

We had differing reactions from our parents. My father-in-law was very supportive and proud that we were able to retire at a relatively young age. He had always told us to "do it as soon as you can". On the other hand, my mother was disappointed. She enjoyed her son being an officer of a prestigious company. She got over it.

We made a mistake during this time that I want to share. We decided to check our medical conditions while still under employer insurance. We did not have any particular problems but visited the doctor, dentist, and dermatologist for check-ups. Nothing significant was found, but we were later dogged by questions during our application for private medical insurance. They wanted to know why we had this recent spate of medical appointments; what was wrong? Our insurer of choice ended up coming to our house and doing a medical check-up of their own, taking measurements, samples, etc. Live and learn.

Before we left work, we discussed what we wanted to do as part of our regular routine those first months. Our beach house had always been a second home, a vacation place. It was outdated and needed renovation. For our transition activity (see Chapter 3), we decided to remodel the beach house ourselves. Neither of us had any real experience doing this work, but we dove in and went from one end of the house to the other. It didn't take a few months; it took us a year and a half. We fell into a typical work routine, with weekends off; however, our normal quitting time became 2:30 in the afternoon (slackers!).

There is an interesting anecdote from that period, occurring about three months into retirement:

We were still in the excitement stage, and cautiously optimistic regarding our financial assumptions, when "life" happened. That summer of 2008, the steepest financial decline since The Great Depression hit the U.S. Financial markets trembled, stocks crashed, government bailouts became a household term, and millions of people lost their jobs. We quickly lost close to one third of our household wealth.

Not a good way to start an early retirement.

Our reaction to this (besides being rattled) was to stay the course. In Chapter 5, we discuss how to diversify your investments so that you are never forced to sell stocks in a "down" market. We had put the proceeds from our house sale into a ladder of CDs; a fixed income, FDIC-insured investment. We were able to live off those CDs until, years later, the market rebounded. Crisis avoided. But I have to say that when you are in the depths of a downturn like that, with no end in sight, it does make for trying times.

There is another instructive anecdote I would like to share. During those first years of retirement, I stayed fairly close to my work friends (still do), and returned to my former workplace for ceremonies, lunches, and other invitations to visit. About a year and a half after I left, the business took a downturn. The Institute began laying people off, a practice almost unheard of for this organization. People I knew were losing their jobs. I couldn't help but think of things I would do differently if I was still working there. The idea of trying to get back involved had a strong allure. But I reminded myself that the people now responsible for the business were my friends. I recommended some of them for their positions. So, I put myself in their shoes. They wanted, and needed, to fix the problems themselves.

I was still connected enough to go back in some official capacity, but it wouldn't have been the right thing to do. Well-intentioned maybe, but being honest with myself, it would have also been my ego wanting to demonstrate how it should be done, at the expense of the people now running the show. I reminded myself that once retired, it's important to make a clean break from work and let the people there do their jobs. The Institute has since recovered from that downturn, without my assistance. Remember the workplace/swimming pool analogy—the hole you leave behind won't last very long.

In Chapter 3, we talk about the importance of developing a list of potential retirement activities. Some of these might be joint activities with a spouse, while others will be yours alone. Below is a sampling of some of the activities on my list, and how they turned out for me.

Boxing—I have always enjoyed sports, including boxing. I had tried my hand at it in Scouting and school, but had no formal training. After I retired, I joined the Corpus Christi Police Officers Association Boxing Team (you didn't need to be an officer to join). I received some formal instruction there and had a couple of amateur fights, including participation in the annual Ringside World Championships in Kansas City, the largest amateur boxing tournament in the world. Cards on the table—I didn't win my fights; I lost two split decisions. But it was highly enjoyable. I got into terrific physical shape and had regular sparring matches every week as part of my training. However, after a year and a half of participation, the linkage between head concussions and CTE (chronic traumatic encephalopathy; i.e., brain damage) became a hot topic. After much consternation, I hung the gloves up. Still enjoy a good heavy-bag workout though.

Pool (Billiards)—I thought that playing pool would be one of my "go-to" retirement activities. It looked good in theory. I liked pool, it was something I could practice on my own, there were competitive leagues nearby, and I had a room in the beach house that could accommodate a full-size pool table. I got the table and put in the effort, but it didn't really work out. I just never found the anticipated enthusiasm for it. Ended up giving the table away to a friend of mine.

Theater—When I was in school growing up, I always enjoyed on-stage opportunities in live theater. Once retired, I got involved with the local theater community and regularly performed where we lived. Later, I performed in a number of regional productions with a different group. When we moved to Alabama, I introduced myself to the local organization and have performed in several productions. Theater has proven to be a core retirement activity for me.

Writing—Another activity that really stuck. In

addition to this non-fiction book, I have written two novels, *Sudden Justice* and *Border Justice* (Oak Tree Press and Amazon). Writing has proven to be one of my favorite retirement pursuits and has the added advantage of complementing my theater efforts. The empathy required to develop characters in novels and on-stage is very similar. Writing is my primary solo activity. I find it enjoyable and always available. I can't really say I have ever been bored in retirement, and writing is one of the big reasons.

Volunteering—At this writing, we have been retired for eleven years. Our volunteer activities were interrupted in year nine (2017) by Hurricane Harvey, when we tore our house down and focused on relocating. We now live in Alabama, on a lake near Birmingham. Our daughter's family (including two grandkids!) live nearby. The activity descriptions below are pre-hurricane, but I have no doubt that we will pick them back up once we are settled in our new locale.

At the beginning of this section, I mentioned my love of animals and early ambition to be a veterinarian. I've taught birds to talk and dogs to count, and very much enjoy our current contingent of three boxers. In retirement, we visit the local animal shelter weekly to take out all their dogs and give them some fun and exercise.

We also enjoy weekly volunteer sessions at the local elementary school. We have worked with second, third, and fifth graders, helping with math, reading, standardized testing, and science lab.

Travel—Another fun retirement pursuit is travel, mainly by car with our three dogs. We enjoy making various loops of the country (e.g., northwest, southwest, southeast) seeing the sights, visiting friends and family, and just enjoying the different environments and people. I have a California brother-in-law who likes to sign me up for some kind of active adventure every time we visit (so far, we've tried skydiving, zip-lining, and tree climbing). We have had good success renting single family vacation homes with fenced yards for our dogs.

Of course, every now and then we get a surprise. On a recent trip to Miami we rented a small home located in a suburban neighborhood of single-family homes. The caretaker of the property told us at check-in that she lived "next door". The first night, my wife swore she heard noises coming from the locked attached garage (we had parked in the driveway head-on to the garage). I went out with the house key, walked around to the side of the house, and opened the side door to the garage. Imagine my shock when I walked in on the caretaker, a middle-aged lady living in a converted garage, getting ready for bed!

W.O.W.

In any field of employment, the most enjoyable position

is one where you have risen to the level of authority, responsibility, and independence necessary to get the job done.

Retiree Interview #2

Vance Braswell

Pell City, Alabama

Vance is 86 years old, married, and a long-time retiree.

What made you decide to retire?

"I was tired of working. I like to work outside, not in a dang store. I had a retail furniture business. There's nothing wrong with people, but having to talk to 'em all the time---I thought I could do better than that. I was tired of tryin' to sell something, or trying to get my troops to sell something. And it was dog eat dog."

Do you regret not working longer?

"Ha! Never. I wouldn't have worked as long as I did, if I could have left sooner."

Was retirement difficult to adjust to?

"No. I was good as soon as I quit."

What kinds of things did you first do, and what do you enjoy doing now?

"Started working in my yard. I have a lot of land, and I like to cut trees, move rocks, work with something heavy. It don't take much brains, but you feel like you're doing something. I like going to the gym —been going since I was in my 30's. Always have done some kind of exercise. I also like a dog. Sometimes you feel like an idiot being a husband."

What are some of the best things about being retired?

"Biggest thing is you get up and start when you want to. I like to get up around six o'clock, sometimes earlier. When I used to work, I would get up at 4, go downtown to the Y, and work out before heading to my job. I like going to the movies sometimes. Always liked Clint Eastwood."

What are some of the worst things about being retired?

"Just gettin' mad because I had to work so long before I got to retire."

Can you offer any advice for people considering retirement?

"Biggest thing keeping people from retiring is money. They worry if they have enough money to retire. Also, you have to find something you like doing. You don't have to adore it, but you need to like it. I don't really like to fish and hunt, except maybe a little squirrel hunting. I do love cars and used to want to race them, but it costs a lot of money. I have owned a lot of nice cars."

**At this point in the interview, a friend of ours, Bobby, walked up to see what we were doing. He is in his sixties and also retired. I put the same question to him:

Any advice for people considering retirement?

"If you don't have something you love to do, it's boring as hell. I'm still lookin' myself. I do try to spend time helping other folks."

What did you used to do?

"I was a welder. I had back trouble and had to retire."

How's your back now?

"It feels better. I've tried to go back to work, but no one will hire me. They're all worried I'm going to have back problems. If I could work again, I would."

CHAPTER 3

BEFORE YOU PULL THE TRIGGER—RETIREMENT PREPARATIONS

Financial Planning and Execution--Savings Accumulation

How Much is Enough?

For most people, the classic "three-legged stool" of retirement income still applies: Personal Savings, Pension/401K, and Social Security.

Funding for both necessities and planned activities is a fundamental requirement for a comfortable retirement. It's true that there are people who survive on Social Security alone, but that program is meant to be a supplement, not a stand-alone source of income.

Long-term savings accumulation should be considered a journey toward financial independence. While working and saving, there is no need to decide how the money will ultimately be used--the goal of financial independence leaves all options open, including retirement. A great benefit of this process is that you will become more comfortable in your job as you wean yourself off the necessity of constant income. You will increasingly be able to function and make decisions for the good of your business without being unduly influenced by personal risk; i.e., fear of losing your job. In other words, your growing income independence will reduce your level of stress and help you to perform your job to the best of your ability.

Now for the big question that everyone asks: If/when I do retire, how much money do I need?

This is a tough question because people are different, things always change, and people adapt differently to change. There is an oft-quoted metric that you should replace 80% of your working income in retirement. While this is a comforting suggestion for financial advisers who profit from the size of your investments, the reality is that expenses will typically be much lower in retirement than in your working years. Increases in health care, entertainment, and travel are more than offset by savings on things like housing, transportation, clothes, taxes, kids, and... savings! That's right, you no longer need to allocate money into savings. Also, you will be able to participate in one of the few advantages of aging--senior discounts (lol).

Let's try and answer the "how much?" question with a reasonable, conservative approach that will get you in the right ballpark.

First, you need an estimate for your annual retirement budget. This should be based on your current spending history, adjusted for the changes discussed above. This will not be an exact science. Using a couple of years of recent credit card and bank statements, you can estimate recurring (regular) expenses. An annual allowance for major expenditures that don't happen each year (new car, roof replacement, etc.) should then be added to these recurring expenses. Next, consider your planned source for retirement healthcare insurance and adjust for any difference. Now, consider specific retirement changes you are planning (e.g., a housing move, children leaving home, etc.) and roll these in to the estimate. Finally, increase your entertainment and travel budget by a fixed percentage (say 30%) and decrease your work-intensive expenses, like transportation and clothes, by a similar percentage. Last step, estimate how much income tax you need to pay to retain this draft budget amount (online tax calculator) and add it in. The resulting number is your Estimated Annual Budget for retirement.

If you decide to fund your retirement by converting your Savings Accumulation (pension/401K and personal savings) into lifetime annuities, and combining that with Social Security, then your "how much?" analysis consists of comparing your Estimated Annual Budget with your projected annual receipts. When making this comparison, consideration should be given to potential inflation (recent historical averages are 1—3% per annum). It should be noted that Social Security already has inflationary adjustments called COLAs (Cost of Living Adjustments) built into the program.

If you are not yet sure about annuitizing your Savings Accumulation, let's make a conservative assumption that will simplify the analysis of how much total money you need to retire. Noting that interest rates generally increase with inflation, let's assume that all earnings on your Savings Accumulation will be used to compensate for inflation plus pay the income taxes on those same earnings. Basically, this assumes all your investment earnings, after taxes, will be used just to keep pace with inflation. In reality, with a modicum of investment success, your earnings should be able to pay these costs and leave money left over, except for rare periods of time (e.g., mid to late 1970s).

Mathematically then:

Earnings on Accumulation = Inflation Adjustment + Taxes on Earnings.

Using this assumption, a simple formula can be used to predict how many years your savings will last:

Savings Accumulation ÷ Estimated Annual Budget = Estimated Years of Retirement Income

As an example, let's suppose you have two hundred thousand dollars in personal savings and another four hundred thousand in a 401K retirement account, and your Estimated Annual Budget in today's dollar value, including income taxes, is $60,000. The number of years you can expect this to last would be 600,000 ÷ 60,000, or about 10 years.

It should be noted that the actual dollar amount of

withdrawals will increase over the years because of inflation, but our assumption mitigates the effect of inflation and allows you to calculate using a constant ($60,000) annual rate of withdrawal.

Also, Social Security will provide roughly one third of a $60,000 annual budget. For our example, this means you really only need to spend $40,000 of your Savings Accumulation each year. Adjusting for this, the number of years you can now expect your money to last would be 600,000 ÷ 40,000 = 15 years. After those 15 years, depending upon the actual rate of inflation and the return on your investments, your $600,000 Savings Accumulation could be exhausted, leaving you with only your Social Security income.

Is 15 years enough? That's a good question. How long do you think you will live?

Life insurance companies hire experts in actuarial science. This discipline studies the statistical probability of people living to a certain age. It's a little bit like a Las Vegas casino. The house (think insurance company) is sure to win in the long run, but they will have some losses along the way (think good genes). You need to consider your current health and genetics (family history) and make your best guess. Only you can decide how many years will make you feel comfortable.

For improved accuracy, the income tax portion of your Estimated Annual Budget should be averaged over the years of retirement. In our example, depending on what account is used for withdrawals, the amount subject to tax will be anywhere between zero and $60,000 (after-tax account without earnings versus deferred tax account). Typical savings accounts are set up with after-tax dollars, so only earnings are subject to taxation. Pensions and 401Ks typically use tax-deferred dollars and therefore 100% of a withdrawal from that account is typically subject to taxation. For any account, taxes will depend upon the mix of after-tax or deferred-tax holdings, taxable and deferred-tax earnings, and type of earnings.

For our example, the tax rate would vary between withdrawals from personal savings (a mix of after-tax dollars and earnings at time of calculation) and a typical 401K (all pre-tax dollars). A worst-case assumption for a conservative first approximation of Income Tax would be to assume all of the $60,000 is taxed as ordinary income. This would be the case if withdrawals were made from a typical pension or 401K retirement account.

Using this assumption in our example, and assuming no state income tax:

Estimated Annual Budget = $60,000

From 2019 On-Line Tax Calculator (Married): Income Tax = $3,884

Estimated Living Expenses = Estimated Annual Budget – Income Tax = $56,116

To consider the effect of different living expense estimates, you can run trials (iterate) with the Tax Calculator to find what estimated annual budget and corresponding income tax provide the desired level of living expense. As in the example above, the new Estimated Annual Budget can then be used to estimate how long your savings will last.

W.O.W.

You will never win an argument with a customer.

Savings Secrets—There are None

Here's an important message:

You don't need a financial advisor. It's just not that complicated.

And remember, middlemen cost. A lot. Over a long time-horizon, such as saving for retirement, investing expenses become a very significant drag on total returns.

If you do decide to hire a financial advisor, I recommend a "fee-for-service" type who charges you a set price or hourly rate for their service. This is in contrast to an "advisor" (stockbroker) who charges for every transaction (buy or sell orders in your account). The latter type has a built-in incentive to "churn"; i.e., maximize transactions in your account regardless of need. Worse still are "advisors" who make a commission on the products (annuities, insurance) they sell to you—a clear conflict of interest. Of specific note, variable annuities are often sold as retirement savings plans; however, they are not a good choice for most investors. They have relatively high fees, a high tax rate on withdrawal (ordinary income versus dividends or capital gains), exposure to potential insurance company bankruptcy, and difficulty in getting out if you change your mind. That said, once you have already accumulated savings and make the decision to retire, annuitizing all or part of your savings for convenient retirement planning and spending may be appropriate.

In this chapter, you will learn the basics of how to put together an effective, conservative savings plan by yourself. But I recommend that you also spend some time getting comfortable with fundamental investing terminology and methods. A subscription to a reputable financial magazine, like Kiplinger's, is a good place to start (there are a number of other readily-available resources to choose from). I would also recommend you begin to regularly read or scan the business section of your selected news source for background and real-world examples of investment strategy.

Once you learn the basics (e.g., asset type/risk, liquidity, diversification, insured vs. uninsured savings, etc.), you will be in position to put together a savings plan that makes sense for you. If you are starting at a fairly young age, say in your early forties or below, slow and steady will win the race. Your investments don't need to be complex; in fact, you should never invest in something that you don't completely understand. Too good to be true is almost always just that. Another fundamental principle is not investing in stocks based on stock market predictions. At any moment in time, market values have already factored in available data from the public domain, including future trends. Without insider information, your odds of predicting something that hasn't already been widely considered are slim.

Home ownership (home equity) remains a common foundation for long-term savings. Once you are confident of staying in one place for at least a few years, you should strongly consider buying a home rather than renting. The cost of renting is typically higher than the net cost of home ownership (equity accumulation minus taxes, maintenance, insurance, and after-tax interest), particularly after a mortgage has been paid down. It's true there have been some notable "housing bubbles" over the years, but long-term appreciation averaging 3-5% is the historical norm. For some, the "forced savings" aspect of monthly mortgage payments requires less budgeting discipline than other savings alternatives.

For someone starting a long-term savings plan, the first priority should be to save three to six months of job income—emergency savings. This money will be your insurance against sudden job loss, and should be invested in insured fixed-income savings, such as FDIC-insured Certificates of Deposit (CDs). Although not a big money-generator, the CDs will produce a guaranteed income and serve their purpose as low-risk, emergency savings. CDs can be purchased through your bank, but the large investment firms that cater to individual investors (e.g., Vanguard and Fidelity) may be a better source. Starting such an account at one of these firms will make it easier to later invest in their mutual fund accounts. Also, CDs purchased in this manner can be easily sold before maturity at market rates. If you purchase them at an individual bank, you will be penalized for early withdrawal. A good strategy to smooth out CD interest rates over time (reduce volatility) is to construct a "CD ladder". This is accomplished by initially buying several CDs with different maturity dates (say 1,2,3, and 4 years). With this strategy, you cash in a CD each year to purchase a new one at prevailing rates.

After emergency savings, your next priority should be to examine your existing debt and work toward its elimination. Apply your available funds in order of biggest impact (highest interest rate/cost), first paying off credit cards and other high-interest loans, then car and student loans, then home equity and mortgage loans. Use credit cards as a convenience, not a loan. Pay the entire balance off each month.

Regarding the available tax deduction for home equity and mortgage loans, it's tempting to think you can make more money by investing rather than paying off the loan; however, it can sometimes be difficult to beat the guaranteed return and simplicity of paying off mortgage debt, particularly when considering the higher income tax standard deduction (after 2018). Additionally, once your mortgage is paid off, your mortgage insurance premium goes away and you will be in control of deciding how much home insurance you need. And there will be no more need to interact with a lender or document the loan on your 1040 tax form each year. A compromise approach is to split your available savings between paying off mortgage debt and starting regular deposits into index mutual funds. Both index mutual funds and tax-advantaged savings should be strongly considered as the foundation of your long-term savings plan.

W.O.W.

If you really need to make sure something gets done, schedule it first thing in the morning.

Index Fund Investing

For most individual investors, a small but diversified mix of index mutual funds makes the most sense for the backbone of their long-term savings plan. Index funds purchase a wide variety of established holdings to mimic market indexes like the S&P 500 (US stocks) or Barclays (US Treasury Bonds) or MSCI (real estate). They are considered "passively-managed", because they don't have to pick and choose their holdings; they just maintain the same general mix of holdings as their market index to provide the broad-market return of that index. This is in contrast to "actively-managed" (or managed) funds, where expert analysts are hired to accurately pick individual winners and losers, and achieve market-beating returns.

Index fund holdings consist of shares across the entire index selected. Managed funds try to be selective and only pick holdings they think will be performance "winners" (high positive returns). The resulting lesser number of holdings in managed funds means that each individual holding has more impact on total returns. Therefore, there is less of an averaging effect, and increased volatility (performance swings). Lessening the emotional roller coaster of volatile returns is one advantage of index funds.

An even greater advantage is lower expenses. It costs money to hire analysts and try to accurately pick and choose market-beating holdings. How much lower are index fund expenses? So much that most managed funds can't make up the difference through improved performance (higher returns).

To sum up, the index fund methodology gives up the chance for market-beating returns in exchange for reduced volatility and a better than even chance to out-perform most managed funds. In fact, research has shown that managed funds fail to beat comparable index funds approximately 70% of the time.

To diversify your investments, you can purchase index funds in most categories (e.g., domestic and international stocks, commercial and government bonds, real estate, etc.) and sub-categories. Diversification among several different categories will reduce volatility by lessening your dependence on any single one.

For a simple start in index fund investing, consider a fund like Vanguard Balanced Index Fund, which provides broad-market exposure to both stocks and bonds (if you own a home, you already have a big investment in real estate). For savings ease, you can set up automatic regular deposits of the same dollar amount. This investing method provides the advantage of "dollar cost averaging"--buying more shares of the fund when the price is lower, and less shares when the price is higher.

W.O.W.

In today's digital world, be more scared of corporate snooping versus government snooping. Google and

Amazon are not your friends.

Tax-advantaged Savings

Regarding tax-advantaged savings, there are opportunities as an individual and there may also be opportunities sponsored by your employer.

As an individual, you can invest a limited amount of money into an IRA (Individual Retirement Account) each year. There are two types of IRA's:

- With a traditional IRA, the taxes on the money you invest, and the earnings it generates, are deferred until you withdraw it (without penalty after age 59 ½). The theory is that your income, and therefore your tax rate, will be lower after retirement.
- With a Roth IRA, you use taxed money to invest, but the earnings grow tax-free; i.e., you pay no taxes on withdrawal (without penalty after age 59 ½).

Your employer may also have a retirement plan option. Some have in-house pension plans; however, these are generally being phased-out for what the federal government calls 401Ks. 401Ks are similar to traditional IRAs in that they provide a way to save on a tax-deferred basis. The big advantage to 401Ks is that your employer may contribute some of their own money into your account. Additionally, the employer may "match" your contribution up to a certain percentage. Generally, you should invest in these 401Ks up to the maximum extent allowed (there are federal limits), and always capture all available employer matching dollars.

Another opportunity for tax-advantaged savings is through state-sponsored 529 plans. These savings plans are like a Roth IRA, allowing your earnings to grow tax-free, as long as they are used for educational purposes (specific limitations and types of schools vary by state). Most people use these plans to save for family college expenses. Similar to 529 plans, Series EE and I bonds issued by the federal government can also be used to accumulate tax-free earnings; however, the benefit only applies when used for higher education, post-secondary institutions.

For qualified health care expenses, there is a way to cut costs by opening a Health Savings Account (HSA). With an HSA, you can make limited contributions of pre-tax dollars, and these dollars are allowed to grow tax-free. Contributions using after-tax dollars are tax-deductible. The idea is that neither the original contribution nor the earnings are subject to federal tax as long as they are used to pay for eligible medical expenses. To qualify, you must be enrolled in a High Deductible Health Plan, defined by IRS minimum limits on individual and family deductibles. If you elect to withdraw money from this account for non-qualified purposes, the money is subject to federal income taxes plus a penalty, unless you are over age 65. Such withdrawals after age 65 are subject to tax, but no penalty.

W.O.W.

It's true. There is real strength in diversity, resulting from exposure to different traits and ideas coupled with Darwinism (survival of the fittest). It's like the longevity of a mongrel dog vs. a pure-bred.

General Notes and Lifestyle Choices

Once you have established a regular savings discipline with index funds and tax-advantaged accounts, and your salary rises over time, make it a goal to save four to six years of your Estimated Annual Budget for retirement in low risk investments (CDs, government bonds, treasury bills, etc.). When needed, this money can be used during stock market downturns instead of having to sell-off stock at low prices. After the downturn has passed, these low-risk funds can be replenished from rebounded stock holdings. They will be the last funds you use in retirement, if/when other accounts have been exhausted.

As a long-term saver, it's helpful and satisfying to put together a simple spreadsheet and track your current and projected savings. This will show your progress toward financial independence and provide an estimate of when you will be financially able to retire.

Let's move on now from the structural discussion of savings and talk a little about lifestyle choices.

Regardless of income, a savings plan will only work if you live within your means. This means having money left over for savings after all living expenses have been paid. After basic needs are met (food, shelter, transportation, healthcare), spending is really a choice.

You should learn to live comfortably, but not lavishly. Economists have a concept called the Law of Diminishing Marginal Utility: as consumption of something increases, the utility (inherent value) gained from consuming additional increments declines. What does this mean to us? Well, after acquiring the basics of something, buying more/bigger/better of the same thing doesn't provide as much satisfaction as the original purchase (think bigger houses and fancier cars). Let's face it, possessions and their infrastructure soak up not just initial cost, but maintenance dollars and time to keep them going. We can learn a lot from the American writer Henry David Thoreau, and his "less is more" lifestyle. I'm not advocating for anyone to go off and live in the woods by himself, like Thoreau did.

We live in a social culture that requires some possessions. But most of us could stand a little "downsizing" and cutting back on our surrounding infrastructure. We should all learn to spend more on the daily pleasures of life, and our loved ones, and less on big assets like fancy homes and cars.

The idea of cutting back and living within our means is difficult for many people. American society is built on consumption, and we are bombarded with advertising, put together by very smart people, that uses every possible ploy to get us to buy. It's important to remind ourselves that self-worth does not equal possessions. We all need to keep in mind our priorities and the big picture of what we want out of life. One of the most impactful decisions you can make in this regard is to avoid hanging around people who compete with each other based on money. Life really is more than being rich in dollars.

The financial heavy-hitters for most of us are our cars and our houses. Personally, I love cars—always have. They're a weakness of mine. But there are some simple principles you can follow to ease their financial burden. You should drive what you like, but keep it longer. Also, pay cash for your cars if you can. As far as houses, the old adage applies: "What are the three most important factors in real estate? Location, location, location." Consider buying a fixer-upper in a good neighborhood and avoid the most expensive house in the neighborhood. Beware of buying a new house in a tract-home subdivision under construction; when you decide to sell you will compete with all the new-builds of similar design.

On the subject of houses, I think it makes sense to consider the purchase of a vacation home, if finances permit. I know we just talked about downsizing, but before you call me a hypocrite, there are some good reasons for this suggestion. If you shop around (see above), the home should appreciate in value over time and be a good financial investment. Look for a home in an area you might consider as your future retirement community. Since you won't yet be there fulltime, look for rental potential, either short-term or long-term (e.g., garage apartment). A home with rental potential can pay its expenses while it appreciates, while you enjoy it in your off-time, and while you discover if it makes sense to retire or sojourn there.

And then there are kids. We just talked about being mindful of our priorities and the big picture of what we want out of life. For many people, their children are at the top of the list. Financially speaking, as soon as you're ready for children, you should try to have them. It's more difficult to save and downsize for retirement while there are still kids at home.

We have discussed tax-advantaged ways to save for college. Your kids can also apply for scholarships and work/study programs. Public universities are almost always less expensive; however, you should be aware that private university tuition is typically not as expensive as you might think. Scholarships are plentiful and full-price tuition is more the exception than the rule. Similar to a car dealership, a "good deal" on tuition can often be found with a small effort.

W.O.W.

The most distinguishing trait of humans versus animals is the ability to document and build upon knowledge through the generations. (And cooking our food!)

Social Security

Social Security can be considered a lifetime annuity (payments until death), periodically adjusted for inflation.

As with any government program, there are numerous exceptions and nuances regarding the rules. In the interest of brevity, this discussion will go over the basics for the vast majority of applicants, neglecting situations outside the norm. For additional details, take a look at the SSA (Social Security Administration) website at socialsecurity.gov.

If you have worked for ten years or more, you are eligible for Social Security benefits.

The dollar amount of your monthly benefit will depend upon:

- Your average monthly earnings during the 35 years you earned the most
- How old you are when you start receiving benefits
- How much you earn if you take benefits and continue working before the SSA "full" retirement age

Benefits (monthly payments) can be started any time after age 62; however, the longer you wait to receive benefits (defer), the larger the benefit is, up to age 70. After age 70, there is no additional benefit resulting from deferral.

For retirees who can afford to defer, the central question is when to start receiving benefits in order to maximize lifetime income.

Research has shown that if you're in good health, have a family history of longevity, and have enough other income so you can wait before taking benefits, it makes sense to defer Social Security benefits until about age 69 to 70.

If you wait until age 70 to take benefits, this decision will begin to pay off after about 8--9 years (age 78—79), at which point the total dollars received approximates the total dollars you would have received had payments started at 62. This is the approximate "breakeven" point; i.e., if you live past 78 —79 you will gain additional income through deferral. This assumes benefits are spent when earned and are not taxed.

Another way to say this: If you are single and take the benefits at age 62, and then die before you reach about age 78--79, you made the right call (more dollars). On the other hand, if you wait to start benefits until age 70, and live past age 78-79, you made the right call (more dollars).

Your odds of living to an old age increase the older you are. For example, a couple where both partners have reached age 65 has a 40% chance that one of them will make 90. A 62-year old male has a life expectancy of about 20 years and a female about 23 years. The deferral strategy makes sense for both married and single people, but is a no-brainer for a married couple because of their joint life expectancy and joint eligibility for the benefit.

Benefits rise about 8% for each year of deferral. The increased lifetime benefit from waiting pays more than you can get by buying a private fixed annuity, due to its automatic adjustments for inflation. Another way to say this: If you tried to buy a fixed lifetime annuity on the open market using the same amount of dollars as a year of deferred Social Security payments, it wouldn't pay back as much as simply taking the increased inflation-adjusted Social Security payments via deferral. You can't get an annuity with a guaranteed 8% return, and inflation protection, for the same money.

If you work while taking Social Security, the benefit

may be subject to significant taxation. Also, if you are less than "full retirement age" (66-67) and keep working while receiving benefit payments, the payments will be reduced if you earn more than a set limit ($17,640 at this writing). If you want to keep working, and can afford it, strongly consider waiting to take benefits (deferral) until you quit, or at least until you attain full retirement age.

Research has shown that for married couples, it usually makes the most sense to have the lesser-earning spouse take benefits earlier and defer the higher-earning spouse benefits. The lesser-earning spouse (usually the wife) will likely live longer and her benefits will be replaced by the larger benefits of the deceased spouse, after his death.

For two married people, the person with the smaller individual benefit has the option of either receiving that, or else half of their spouse's higher benefit.

In summary, and on average, to maximize lifetime income: If you are a married man or single woman, and can afford it, defer taking benefits until about age 69. Married women should take benefits early at age 62. Single men, if they can afford it, should strongly consider deferral, although the decision is not as clear-cut as for married men.

One last question we should consider before leaving the Social Security discussion. We have talked about the best strategy to maximize lifetime income received from Social Security. But there is another consideration here.

As we age, we tend to slow down in most things. If you delay taking Social Security benefits (defer), will you enjoy the resulting extra income in your 70s and beyond as much as you would have enjoyed the reduced, but still significant, benefit starting at age 62?

Something to think about.

W.O.W.

Accept your limitations and age gracefully, but before you give something up that has become difficult with age, be really sure you can't do it anymore. Once you give it up, chances are you'll never do it again.

Health Insurance

Health insurance is a necessity in the United States. Without it, there is a very real risk of bankruptcy in the event of serious illness.

For the vast majority of retirees age 65 and older, the government program Medicare serves as their primary medical insurance. With some exceptions (e.g., if you are already receiving Social Security benefits), you must make a timely application for Medicare with the SSA around your 65th birthday, or face penalties. In addition to Medicare, you may also be able to leverage medical coverage offered through your former workplace.

Retirees under the age of 65 have the option of private medical insurance. This can be expensive; however, keeping the deductibles high (catastrophic coverage) can lower the cost. For these high-deductible plans, Health Savings Accounts can provide additional cost savings (see Chapter 3). Also, high-deductible plans of large insurers deliver pre-negotiated discount pricing for all healthcare services. Don't be fooled into thinking that if you forego insurance and pay cash for everything, you're going to get the cheapest rates.

With the advent of the Affordable Care Act (Obamacare), there is now another option for early retirees. Generally, if your Adjusted Gross Income (AGI) on IRS Form 1040 is between one and four times the federal poverty level for your size family unit, you are eligible for health insurance subsidies in the form of tax credits. Depending on where you fall within this range, and which specific health plan you select, the subsidies may cover the entire cost of your health insurance. This is an excellent option for early retirees funding retirement from personal savings using after-tax dollars. Early retirees in this situation can facilitate eligibility by investing a portion of their savings in a tax-managed index fund. This will reduce earnings impact on AGI and help maintain income within the specified range of eligibility.

It should be noted that the Affordable Care Act has become a political football and is under assault from a variety of sources. There is no way to know how it will evolve in the coming years.

W.O.W.

Aging is like a recurring rust that can be knocked loose with physical and mental activity. Don't quit on something physical just because you're a little stiff starting out.

Lifestyle Visualization and Experimentation

For retirement planning, it's necessary to focus on finances, but it's just as important to focus on lifestyle decisions. Finances provide the means for retirement, but how you spend your time will determine your satisfaction.

You should try out potential retirement locales and interests while you are still working. Using personal leave for this purpose has limitations, so if you have an opportunity to shift to part-time work in advance of full retirement, strongly consider it. This is an excellent way to allocate significant time to lifestyle experimentation before making a final retirement decision.

It's important (and fun!) to visualize and document

the things you might like to do in retirement.

Consider all the things that you enjoy doing now.

Write 'em down.

Now go back and consider all the things that you used to enjoy doing when you were younger and didn't work fulltime, including school activities. Consider the electives you took in high school and college. There was a reason you picked those classes. Perhaps there were also extracurricular courses and activities that you liked.

Write 'em down.

Now think of all the things that you think you might enjoy doing if you had the time and money. Include possible volunteer activities. You may have never tried these things before. That's okay.

Write 'em down.

The document resulting from this exercise will become your working Potential Activities List for retirement--your PAL! (lol)

Update it often as you consider new ideas from reading, media, entertainment, trial, and experimentation. Not everything on this list will become a retirement activity, but many will. If you have a spouse or partner, some of these interests may turn into joint activities, but it's important that some of them don't. You and your spouse will likely be together more than ever during retirement, and you each need some pursuits that will allow a measure of individual space and freedom.

In Chapter 5, we will look at sojourning—living temporarily in a different place. While you're still working, you should consider potential future retirement locations (permanent or 2nd home) other than your current home. Use some of your off-time to travel there, explore, and understand the real estate market in the area.

If this sounds appealing, you can consider purchasing such a home now, as a vacation home. Earlier, we discussed how to buy such a property and enjoy it in your off-time, at little or no cost. If you decide to go this route, consider finding and hiring a handyman to keep up the yard and fix things that break, so you can use your time there to fine-tune your PAL. Of course, home maintenance may be one of the things already on your PAL, so this becomes a real win-win. Just don't let my wife know there are people like you out there!

W.O.W.

The mind and body decay without demands placed on them. Without exercise, they wither away, along with your self-confidence. Before you know it, a trip to a dinner party becomes uncomfortable—physically and emotionally. Some relaxation is beneficial, but to live a fulfilling life, sloth must be resisted.

Emotional Preparation

In Chapter 1, we discussed some of the emotional considerations that go into the retirement decision. As a final preparation before you pull the trigger, do a little honest introspection and ask yourself the following:

Do you catch yourself pretending to be something you're not?

Do you nag yourself by second-guessing your actions?

Is work an escape mechanism to avoid things that are uncomfortable? Do you "lose yourself" in your work?

These are all common things that people sometimes do. However, when they become standard behavior, it can be indicative of problems at home or a lack of understanding and trusting yourself. It's important to address these issues, particularly when approaching retirement. If you think some of these things may apply to you, recognize what is happening and carve out some quiet time (maybe start with a daily walk) to re-connect with yourself.

Try to compartmentalize your work activities away from your home life (outside interests). The resulting balance and separate home life you develop will allow a future segue into retirement. Without this balance, retirement will be difficult, at least initially. The absence of a satisfying home life leads to anxiety about leaving work and the question so many people fear: "What am I going to do with myself?"

In order to retire successfully, you need to have a positive attitude toward the decision. This does not mean that you have no feelings of fear or uncertainty about what lies ahead. Of course you do. But you should also have an underlying sense of adventure--an excitement about initiating a new phase of life, experiencing new things, and having the freedom to chart your own course every day. You've worked hard to get to this point and now have the opportunity to retire. You no longer need to prove how "successful" you are to yourself or anybody else.

And for early retirees, accept the fact that you are different and it's perfectly fine to do your own thing while most people your age are still working. You should feel proud of your retirement; after all, you've earned it.

W.O.W.

Groupthink is the enemy of freedom.

A Little Help From Your Friends (or not)

Most of your friends will readily accept your decision, congratulate you, and wish you the very best.

It may or may not be something that they want to do, but they're supportive of your decision and happy for you. Some of them may envy your decision and look forward to the day when they can retire. Others may envy your decision, but are too afraid to make such a drastic change themselves. Some are happy in their work, but find it interesting that retirement can be the right choice for others. Other well-meaning friends may think that some circumstance has recently changed: you are being forced to resign; you are ill; you are wanting to start your own business; etc.

If you are an "early" retiree (younger than age 65), you will likely run across some people who feel threatened by your decision. These people may be close acquaintances with whom you've always had a good relationship. We touched on this phenomenon earlier, but it warrants additional consideration. Understanding its motivation will help you deal with it.

As we discussed in Chapter 1, there are always going to be people who are truly happy working at their job until (hopefully) the day they die, regardless of their need for money. These people need their job for various emotional reasons, some noble and some not so noble (e.g.; enjoyment, belonging, purpose, puritan work ethic, staying active doing something they are comfortable and familiar with; and for some, power, prestige, competitive success and self-worth as measured in dollars, fear of being bored and alone).

Some of these people may question your decision: "You're too young to retire." This is a common reaction that sometimes is just meant to convey that you don't fit the norm, or maybe you look younger than most retirees. However, If the person continues down this track, they may feel your decision represents a more personal challenge to their view of acceptable behavior. For instance, they might add: "Are you just going to play around all day?" Translation: you haven't paid your dues yet; it's dishonorable to quit work while you're still healthy; you're being irresponsible, even irreligious.

This type of person feels that early retirement is a rejection of life's core value. Their identity and self-worth are inseparably linked to their job. Someone willing to quit work while still relatively young is seen as a challenge to everything that they believe to be important and essential to a successful and honorable life. To congratulate or admire such an individual would be an affront to their value system. For them, work and the possessions obtained through work are the only true measure of success. Their years of service on the job are a badge of honor; the more years, the higher the honor. And, of course, it is an honor, but not one that everyone needs to pursue. But they feel that to reject this pursuit is a personal affront and, in a way, "unfair". Kind of like cutting in line to get to the happiness/ fulfillment counter. Luckily, these people are few in number. Understanding them makes them easier to deal with.

In the end, it doesn't really matter what these people think. No one has the right to tell you when you can retire. It only matters what you, your loved ones, and your close friends think--and all these people will come to understand and stand behind your decision.

W.O.W.

Why don't journalists have an accreditation group, like doctors or engineers? Anyone could still publish anything, but at least people would know if they adhered to ethical standards (e.g., honesty).

Transition Planning (first six months to a year)

You should have a well-thought-out plan for the first period of retirement.

Once the initial euphoria, retirement party, and excitement wear off, you will be ready to jump in to this new life you've been thinking about for so long.

After many years of a structured workplace lifestyle, it has become an expectation to wake up each day and know what you are going to do. As you progress into your "second life" and develop some of the passions on your retirement list, your emotional dependence on this structured routine will diminish. To facilitate this transition and avoid the initial "What am I gonna do today?" questions, it's a good idea to plan out some desirable activities for that very first stretch of retirement. These can be a mix of temporary actions with end dates, coupled with a few things from your PAL (Potential Activities List) that have more long-term potential.

The temporary activities could consist of a home re-model, a car restoration, a trip around the world, a golfing expedition in an RV, or the start of a part-time consulting position.

Part-time work, including cutting back from your existing job, is an excellent transition strategy. It maintains a measure of structure and familiarity while freeing up some time for PAL experimentation.

This transition period should not be underestimated. After working for many years, it is not a simple thing to "turn the switch" and settle into retirement living. You need time to adjust and mentally process the change. This transition time can be very enjoyable; it just needs to be filled with a core activity or two that you can lean on while you discover some permanent passions to build your "second life" around. And who knows? You may find that some of those initial temporary activities become something more, a part of your regular retirement rhythm.

W.O.W.

There can be no debate without truth as a foundation. Truth is absolute. There are alternative points of view based on the same facts, but there are no such things as alternative facts (alternative truths).

Retiree Interview #3

Curt Friedland

Austin, Tx.

Age 64, Single, Owner of Friedland + Briggs Commercial Real Estate Appraisers

I know you're still working right now. When do you plan to retire?

"If I have my way, I'd like to retire next year when I'm 65. 66 at the latest."

Why have you decided to retire rather than continue working?

"You know, I'm just tired of the daily grind of my business. Even though I'm still interested in it, it's just the day-to-day repetition; knowing that I have to come do this every single day."

Are you planning to gradually transition from

work, or just do it?

"Gradually. I'm planning to reduce my hours over the course of the next year."

Any immediate, short-term plans on what you want to do with your time once you step away?

"A lot of travel, with a focus on Hawaii. That's where I want to end up. I'd like to live there long-term."

How about long-term plans?

"I think that I want to do a couple of real estate pro-jects. Maybe some people wouldn't consider that retirement, but I want to retire from what I'm doing now and do some different things. On the low-end, I want to buy a condo, remodel it, and then flip it. On the higher end, I want to re-develop an existing commercial property. I want to do these projects for the fun of it and also the money—about 50/50. I know this sounds kinda big-headed, but I think Ha-waii can use my input. There's so much troubled real estate there, I just think I can demonstrate how to make something out of it. I really think I can help the city of Honolulu."

Are you confident in your financial planning?

"I feel pretty good about it, but I'm not an expert. I'm constantly seeking knowledge in that area, to improve myself. I'm trying to focus on it more, study up on it."

Any advice for people considering retirement?

"Do it. Do it. Like Nike. Just do it. As long as you're capable of it, financially and psychologically. If you can't have hobbies, or do some other work, then I don't know that it's good."

CHAPTER 4

**ONE MORE TIME—IS THIS SOMETHING I WANT?
A PRE-RETIREMENT QUIZ**

Okay.

We've gone through the pros and cons. We know that retirement is not for everyone.

But is it right for you?

Now that you've had some time to consider how your personal situation relates to what you've read, try answering these questions. In each case, pick the answer that comes closest to describing how you feel:

1) Does the idea of retirement a) excite you, or b) tie your stomach into knots

2) Do you see retirees as a) fortunate, or b) no longer relevant

3) Deciding for yourself how to spend your time is a) liberating, or b) overwhelming

4) Without your job, your self-respect would

a) not really change, or b) suffer

5) Is your job a) boring and repetitive, or b) challenging with opportunities for personal growth

6) Do you see retirement as a

a) chance at a "second life", or

b) the beginning of the end

I think you already know which people are in the "a"

camp and which are in the "b" camp.

If you find that you are more of an "a" type of gal/guy, please keep reading. It's time to talk about living a fulfilling retirement life!

W.O.W

If you were trying to program/educate an all-purpose android to sell anywhere in the world, and were limited to three subjects beyond language and mathematics, what subjects would you choose?

My Picks: Psychology, science (physics/biology/chemistry), economics

Retiree Interview #4

Theresa Harris

Cropwell, Alabama

Theresa is in her mid-sixties and married to husband Ronnie. She retired at an early age and has since gone back to work.

How long were you retired?

"I stayed retired eleven years."

What made you decide to retire?

"We wanted to do our traveling and other life experiences while we were still young enough and healthy enough to enjoy it. We both watched our parents as they got older and when they finally reached retirement age, they just didn't feel like doing anything. Ronnie's father retired and died that same year. That was kind of an eye-opener for us, and we decided that once we could afford to retire, we were going to do it and then make life decisions after that."

Was retirement difficult to adjust to?

"Yes, because none of our friends were retired. So it was extremely difficult. From a social standpoint, it was difficult because we wanted to travel, and had the means to travel, and would have liked to have done it with many of our friends, but our friends were still working. So that made it a little more complicated."

What did you enjoy doing when you were retired?

"Well, travel was at the top of the list for us. Then, I know it's basic, but doing house work and yardwork that we didn't have time to do when we worked. That was pretty important. I also took some classes, like the Master Gardener class, that I could never have done if I was employed because my job required lots of hours. And my job required lots of travel, so I got to spend more time at home, or if I did travel, it was for pleasure."

Why did you decide to go back to work?

"Actually, it was decided for me; I don't think I decided it. Ronnie was asked to help get a company out of trouble with his Human Resources expertise, and when he did that it just happened to be a coincidence that our church was in trouble from a financial standpoint. They asked me if I might step in and try to get their books in order. It just grew from there. I don't think we ever had intentions of going back to work, but the opportunity just kind of hit us that we had been retired for eleven years and we were thinking: "How do we expand our minds, and stay current with modern technology and things like that?" So we both went back to work within months of each other. We had long talks on whether to do it or not, and realized that it wasn't going to work unless both of us did it. Ronnie's job was supposed to last six months and mine was volunteer. I didn't even get paid. So it was going to be for six months and then we were done, but now here we are. Nine years later and I'm still working (Ronnie has since re-retired). I love it. I get to stay up to date on computers and the new technology that's happening, and I enjoy that."

What would you say were the best and worst things about retirement?

"I can tell you the worst. The worst thing was being away from the people I worked with. Definitely the worst part of it. Missing the people, missing the camaraderie of an office staff. The best part is just having the freedom. Freedom to make decisions and go and do as you please. But you know that freedom doesn't come unless you have financial security. And even going back to work, that's why the decision was easy because if I don't like it, I know I can leave. It takes the stress away."

Any advice for people considering retirement?

"Talk with a financial advisor. Maybe even a counselor, not just an advisor but a counselor. A lot depends on if your spouse is retiring, or if you're married or not. The emotional side of it. I think age is a big thing. I was 45 when I retired and people thought I was crazy. Then when Ronnie and I did all our traveling and what we wanted to do, they didn't find it that crazy. And now that we're at that age where we could be retired and traveling, I'm not sure we have the energy to do it all. I would do it again exactly the same way. I wouldn't change a thing."

CHAPTER 5

AND WE'RE OFF!—LIVING THE DREAM

Finally.

Let's fast-forward and assume the big day has arrived. All the preparations have been made, the party at work is finished, and you're ready to start this new chapter of your life.

Let's presume you're leaving work with no plans to go back part-time. When you make that final break, make it a clean break. The workplace is no longer your responsibility. Hopefully, it has been left in capable hands, and now those people need the freedom to do their jobs without you looking over their shoulders. For you, the workplace is now a social place to keep up with old friends.

Long-term, your goal should be to try-out the ideas on your PAL, and identify those that really resonate--that become things you want to do regularly. These are the things that will help you establish a new rhythm and structure to your life. This new structure will be nowhere near as rigid as a typical workplace routine, but it will provide a desirable selection of daily things to do. As these passions develop, you will have less and less a need for temporary transition activities or part-time work.

Give special priority to trying out those activities on your PAL that have a long-term horizon and that you can do solo (e.g., writing, wood-working, painting, etc.). These will be potentially valuable as "go-to" default activities that can always be done and enjoyed; something you can pick up and put back down again until the next opportunity.

You are now able to devote more time and money to your loved ones. One of the great joys of retirement is the opportunity to spend time with family in a free country that has such a wide variety of things to do and places to go.

Now that you don't have to worry about conforming to workplace standards, feel free to relish your individuality. As we age, we tend to care less about what other people may think or say about us. This is a natural process and a good thing. After all, we're all human, we're all a little bit different from each other--a little bit eccentric at heart.

There is no longer a need to strive for conformity; you are your own boss.

W.O.W.

When dealing with a customer, try to "under-promise"

and "over-deliver".

Transition Activities—The First Months of Retirement

We have already discussed the change from fulltime work to retirement and the value of an activity plan for those first months. What we haven't talked about is the joyful experience of this "honeymoon" period.

Regardless of how you decide to spend your time, this will be something you will always remember. Doing your own thing on a permanent basis is pretty heady stuff. The feelings of excitement and freedom are very real. The change is so significant that it may even feel a bit surreal.

My wife and I really enjoyed the whole transitional experience, especially the adventurous mindset of trying out new things. I felt very fortunate to live the retirement lifestyle while I still had good health. In this regard, I was influenced by the experience of my father who died at age 64. He was very much looking forward to retired life, but got cancer before he left work. In the middle of six surgeries, he felt well enough to retire, and did, but died shortly thereafter.

I can still remember telling my wife after that first year: "If I died tomorrow, I would die a happy man with no regrets." And I meant it.

W.O.W.

Religion can corrupt faith and spirituality.

Establish a Rhythm and Give Yourself Permission to Relax

A hurdle to establishing your new retirement rhythm--the loose structure of daily activities that you enjoy--is overcoming the workplace mindset of always needing to be productive. You will have difficulty enjoying yourself until you realize that you don't need to always be productive.

GIVE YOURSELF PERMISSION TO RELAX.

Maybe a part of your desired routine is taking an afternoon nap. Maybe you like to read a few chapters before getting out of bed. Maybe you want to take a walk with your dog. Whatever the "non-productive activity" is, unless it's illegal, harmful to yourself or others, or keeps you from doing things you need to do, work with yourself to get rid of any guilt you may feel from doing it.

Have fun often. Kick the work habit and mindset and do what you want.

During your transition period and through the first year or so of retirement, you will find that you greatly enjoy some of the activities on your retirement list, while others not as much as you thought you would. From the activities that you truly enjoy, you can begin to piece together a loose structure of daily and weekly activities; e.g., Monday go to gym, grocery shop, work on book; Tues jog, volunteer at animal shelter, finish house project, etc.

While a bit of structure can be enjoyable and comforting, be sure to maintain your flexibility and sense of adventure. The freedom to do new things and "spread your wings" is a big advantage of being retired. Whatever daily or weekly structure you come up with, it should be loose enough to easily adjust and take advantage of opportunities that present themselves.

Aging and the freedom to do what you want comes with some responsibility. You have to have the self-discipline to continue to participate in social activities, take reasonable risks, and challenge yourself, so you don't become too "set in your ways". The comfort of home can become so inviting that some people may not want to leave it for trips, shows, social events, etc. They allow a degree of sloth to set in and become bored; worse, they can become depressed or develop a social anxiety.

Stay fit (see Chap 6) and stay engaged in the activities you love.

W.O.W.

In business, never argue against safety or quality. It's like being in politics and not supporting the military—

you will lose.

Pull Out That List and Try Something New

We have discussed the generation of a Potential Activities List (PAL) to guide you in the early stages of retirement. This is a living document that gets things added to it and subtracted from it over time. Once you have experimented with most of the ideas on the list and identified those things that truly interest you, the need for a formal document will expire. New ideas can be addressed as they come up.

The variety of activities available is almost limitless, and the inclusion of any particular activity on your PAL is a matter of personal taste.

There are a couple of items, however, that make their way onto most PALs. Due to their more universal appeal, they deserve special consideration.

W.O.W.

A leader is someone who receives too much credit when things go well, and too much blame when they don't.

Volunteering

Retirement provides an opportunity to use some of your time for "giving back" to your community.

Maybe you enjoy children and can lend a hand at your local elementary school. Maybe you enjoy pets and can help at the Animal Shelter. There are a multitude of possibilities that can be tailored to fit your cause and your schedule. Most volunteer opportunities can be initiated with a simple phone call or personal visit.

A word of caution here: Be wary of becoming wrapped up in administrative duties and getting away from the things you enjoy (unless you enjoy performing administrative duties). For example, if you enjoy gardening and you join the local Garden Club so that you can get outside, meet people, and provide hands-on help to beautify the area, you need to think twice before using your time commitment to perform the duties of Club Treasurer. This is one of those instances where you have to learn to say no.

Every organization has some kind of management structure and recurring administrative tasks. Unless those activities are what you are looking for, stay true to the reasons you volunteered in the first place. This is not a job. You are giving away your time to support a cause and it will be greatly appreciated, regardless of your participation in administrative activities.

Volunteering can also provide the opportunity to socialize with younger people, which is healthy for you and keeps you feeling young and engaged with the world.

W.O.W.

In business, keep rules, bureaucracy and organizational levels to an absolute minimum. Try to keep lines of communication as direct as possible between customer and provider. Bureaucracies grow and middlemen cost.

Travel

You will likely enjoy the freedom you now have to travel at your leisure. Longer trips away from home that were once unfeasible are now possible. Driving trips where you can take your pets along are real options. Day or overnight trips to explore your local region are also fun. The emergence of vacation rental websites like Homeaway and AirB&B allow you to rent a nice home in the area of your choice for a reasonable cost.

On a personal note, we have enjoyed making longer trips of four to six weeks and visiting different sections of the country. Often, we can combine these tours with visits to friends and relatives along the way. A word of advice based on personal experience: When visiting people you know, strongly consider renting a nearby home, or staying at a local hotel, rather than accepting invitations to stay inside the homes of the people you are visiting. A night or two may be fun, but beyond that is an imposition on your host, even if they insist it is not.

Family is important at any stage of life, and in retirement you will want to maintain great relationships with your children and other relatives. With good health and no work schedule, you now have the opportunity to help them in ways that were previously not possible (think grandchildren!) and enjoy their company without being a burden to them. For example, we rented a house in North Carolina for four months after the birth of our first grandchild, babysitting during our kid's transition back to work.

Also, we all love our pets, but perhaps even more so in retirement. They don't replace our children, but they make excellent companions and join us in so many of the things we do. They also are motivational for staying active and getting outside.

W.O.W.

Physical fights are something to never start but always finish.

Sojourning (second home)

If finances permit, you may enjoy having a second home. A second home can provide the means to be closer to family that live elsewhere, escape harsh winter or summer weather, or just provide a refreshing change of pace, scenery, and people.

Maintenance of a second home will always be an issue, so be sure you either enjoy doing the work yourself, have a handyman on-call, or select a low-maintenance property (garden home, condo, or townhome).

As mentioned earlier, it's possible to purchase a second home with rental potential to offset your costs. The strategy could be to rent the property when you're not using it, or to have continuous long-term rental of part of the property (e.g., a garage apartment). Successful rental of a property will be highly dependent on the quality of the tenant. With our beach house, we had long-term tenants in the garage apartment for the first twelve years of ownership—while we still worked. Our rental experience ranged from great (business rental for workers laying fiber optic cable during the week--automated payment of rent, they were gone on the weekends, had a contract service maintain the yard, and remodeled the apartment at their cost), to not so great (private party skipped town leaving damage and rent owed).

The best way to check out prospective tenants, other than finances, is to talk to their past landlords.

W.O.W.

Some lessons can be perfectly explained through words, but not fully understood without experience (e.g., "The Grass is Always Greener").

Retirement Finances

In retirement, you change your financial focus from accumulation to spending. It's important to select the proper accounts from which to withdraw money. This will depend on the type of assets you own and prevailing economic conditions. Also, you should conduct an annual check to verify the adequacy of your savings accumulation.

W.O.W.

Racial discrimination is not okay, cultural discrimination is (if that culture encourages harmful behavior).

Spending and Budgeting

Retirement funding typically comes from a combination of Social Security, pension/401K, and personal savings. Let's take a general look at how best to access these accounts during retirement.

There are no investment account choices necessary to receive Social Security Administration benefits. Your benefit comes directly from the federal government according to your personal situation, work history, and the SSA algorithm. Social Security is a lifetime annuity; i.e., you will continue to receive the monthly benefit for as long as you live.

For a pension or 401K account, there is a good chance that you will need to decide how your money is invested and how you will receive it. Most people annuitize these accounts so that they have a lifetime income, typically with some minimum amount guaranteed. For a fixed lifetime annuity, there is no decision to make regarding which account to draw money from; however, for a variable annuity, the amount you receive will change depending upon the performance of the underlying assets. Typically, you decide what type of assets these are, and accept the impact of that decision on risk and return. Just like when you were accumulating savings, lower-risk assets or guaranteed minimum performance come with the likely trade-off of lower returns over time.

If a significant part of your retirement money comes from personal savings spread out among different classes of assets (stocks, bonds, CDs, etc.), you need to consider how best to withdraw funds. In general, higher risk stock funds should be used during "bull" (rising) stock markets, and fixed income/low risk funds (e.g., CDs, bonds, insured savings) should be used in "bear" (falling) stock markets. After using some of your fixed income funds during a bear market, and following a return to bull market conditions, you should reallocate your remaining funds to maintain a 3—5 year buffer of fixed income/low-risk assets. This buffer should keep you from having to sell-off devalued stocks during a market downturn. (Historically, the average bear market lasts about a year, and then takes about two more years to recover the losses.) This strategy allows you to keep maximizing investment returns rather than switching all your funds to low-risk/low-return based solely on age ("target funds"). The 3—5 year buffer should be the final retirement funds you spend, after exhausting your higher risk stock market investments.

As an emergency stopgap strategy, your home can be used for end-of-life income by selling it and then renting, or by renting out part of it, or by selling it and downsizing to a smaller home, or by giving ownership of your house to a financial institution in exchange for monthly payments and use of the home for the rest of your life (reverse mortgage). A reverse mortgage will result in some lost value for your heirs; however, any remaining mortgage debt will not affect your estate.

W.O.W.

You know things are bad when people say things could be worse.

Lifestyle Decisions

There are a number of cost advantages that come

with not working. For example, you can live outside daily commuting distance from the city; you can eat out during discount times; and you can live in places where jobs are not as prevalent. Generally, if you do things when and where working people can't; you'll save dollars and avoid crowds.

If contemplating an out-of-state move, be sure to include taxes (property, sales, and income) in your decision-making process.

Consider cutting back on infrastructure you used for working; e.g., work clothes, fancy cars, expensive phone plans, etc. If you're not sure about some of these items, try living without them a while to determine if you still need or want them.

Don't be afraid to spend money on yourself and your loved ones. One of the biggest joys in retirement is doing the things you want with your newly-available time. Funding for these activities should be a significant part of any retirement budget.

For many people, spending money on themselves can be a problem, even though they can afford it. After a lifetime of saving and bargain-hunting, frugality can become an ingrained habit and part of a person's identity, making it difficult to spend money even when it's available and there are things they want. Of course, no one likes to be price-gouged no matter how rich they are; but aside from that, if you want something, and you can afford it, you should get it.

Your financial goals and metrics are different at age 65 versus age 45. Assuming your family doesn't need to inherit all your money, learn how to enjoy those hard-earned dollars. That's what they're good for. Before leaving this topic, spend some time and think through your family's situation before you decide to give your kids a lot of money when you die or before you die. Early inheritance can sometimes lead to spoiled kids who are incapable of independent living. Just knowing that they stand to inherit big money can compromise their relationship with you. In addition to family, there will always be worthy causes that could benefit from a bequest.

W.O.W.

Right before a major planned confrontation (battle), there is always an eerie silence.

Measure Results

In Chapter 3, we discussed using a very conservative assumption that the earnings you receive on your retirement accumulation will be consumed by paying the taxes on those earnings along with inflation costs. With this assumption, we were able to do a simple approximation of how many years your accumulation will last:

Accumulation ÷ Estimated Annual Budget = Estimated Years of Retirement Income

Accumulation: An important check on the financial execution of your retirement is an annual assessment of your Accumulation. This is the dollar value of all your assets that could be liquidated without requiring replacement. As such, your necessary infrastructure of home, cars and possessions should not be included in Accumulation. However, if you are still making loan payments on a house (home mortgage), housing is a budgeted expense item and your accrued home equity should be included as part of Accumulation, because it could be sold (second mortgage) without affecting your use of the house.

Estimated Annual Budget: During retirement, you should periodically check your Estimated Annual Budget. An easy way to set this up is to withdraw your annual budget estimate into an easily accessible money market or bank account (spending money), then use it for all purchases that year. At the start of the next budget year, check the account balance and see how much was actually spent. The number should be adjusted for any large anomalous unplanned purchases or changes in a given year. This exercise can be repeated over the course of several years, allowing you to average out some of the infrequent purchases and improve the estimate.

As part of the Accumulation assessment, it is instructive to put together an estimate of your total

Net Worth. The following page is a sample of a Net Worth Estimate (Net Worth = Assets – Liabilities/ Debt), with an additional calculation of asset diversification. This sample estimate assumes no balance of unsecured debt, like a credit card or medical bill balance (mortgage debt is secured/backed by your home value). Only the equity in your necessary infrastructure (percentage of total value that you own), should be included.

For simplicity, the following example only includes the major infrastructure of home and car, and assumes they are paid for (fully owned). Monthly expenses are not a part of this tabulation; the Net Worth Estimate is a snapshot in time of total monetary wealth. I like to keep the entire calculation on a single page for ease of understanding and utility, but it could be expanded:

NET WORTH AS OF 1/1/20 (excludes minor infra-structure/possessions)

AMOUNT	TYPE	AVG%/YR	LIQUID	RISK
350	Home	3	Poor	Low
200	401Kfxd	3	Good	Low
300	401Kstk	7	Good	Med/High
100	Bal Indx	5	Good	Med
50	Int Bond	3	Good	Low
50	500Indx	7	Good	Med/High
40	REITIndx	5	Good	Med/High
40	IntGrow	8	Good	High
40	IRA	5	Poor	Med
60	I Bonds	2	Good	Low
20	Ckg Acct	1	Good	NA
20	Car	--	Good	High

$1,270,000—Estimated Net Worth (3% > 2019 estimate of $1,233,000)

DIVERSIFICATION—31% Real Estate (Home,

REIT)38% Stock (401K stock, .6Bal, 500, Intl, IRA)12% Bonds (.4Bal, Int Bond, I Bonds)16% Comm Insured Savlngs (401K fixed)3% FDIC Insured Savings & Misc (Ckg Acct, Car)

The headers on the Net Worth worksheet are:

Amount—how many dollars, in thousands, contained in account

Type—account description; e.g., Bal Index for a balanced index mutual fund

Avg%/yr—average annual percentage return on account

Liquid—liquidity; ease of converting the account value to cash

Risk—relative chance of losing value; volatility

The worksheet should be updated annually to show how net worth is trending through the years. As part of the annual update, diversification is reviewed and allocations changed, if necessary, to maintain a mix of investments with acceptable risk. Maintaining diversification—investing in different asset classes--will tend to mitigate volatility and provide a more consistent rate of return.

You can use the worksheet to update the Estimated Years of Retirement Income number. First, if fully owned, remove the major infrastructure value of home and vehicle from Net Worth to arrive at Accumulation. Remember, these are items that would have to be replaced, if sold. Of course, the house value could be included as part of Accumulation if you decided to sell it and rent (rental expense would have to be added to your Estimated Annual Budget).

With an updated Accumulation (Net Worth minus necessary infrastructure) and an Estimated Annual Budget, you can calculate an updated value for Estimated Years of Retirement Income:

Accumulation ÷ Estimated Annual Budget = Estimated Years of Retirement Income

In our example above, and using $60,000 as an Estimated Annual Budget:

($1,270,000 - $350,000 - $20,000) ÷ $60,000 = 15 years

If we assume that Social Security benefits have started, and they amount to $2,000/month or $24,000/yr, the annual amount we need to withdraw from the Accumulation goes from $60,000 to $36,000. Now the Estimated Years of Retirement Income is:

($1,270,000 - $350,000 - $20,000) ÷ $36,000 = 25 years

Social Security benefits continue until you die and are automatically adjusted for inflation. In this example, 40% of the Estimated Annual Budget is provided by Social Security.

Besides checking that retirement savings appear adequate, the Net Worth worksheet has the added benefits of showing if your total wealth is increasing or decreasing, the risk level of your portfolio, and the diversification across asset classes. Also, by maintaining a current picture of your financial status on a single page, someone would be able to quickly understand your investments in the event you become seriously ill or die.

W.O.W.

How do you eat an elephant (or attack a big problem)? One bite at a time.

Retiree Interview #5

JoLynn Black

Lewisville, Texas

Jo is in her early sixties, single, and retired four years ago.

What made you decide to retire?

"I was working in an environment where everybody was Type A. You came in early, you stayed late, and you always thought if I just worked a little bit harder today maybe tomorrow would be easier—but it never was. I was already on a couple of medicines for blood pressure and cholesterol, and was about to have to go on pre-diabetes medicine. It occurred to me that I was going to die there if I kept working at this pace."

Any regrets now about not working any longer?

"None. Before I retired, I got with my financial advisor and used his estimates of what my retirement would be, and he promised me that although he didn't have a crystal ball, if all things stayed fairly steady, I was going to be fine."

Before you left work, did you know the things that you wanted to do in retirement?

"People had told me that I needed to have a plan. They said to plan in some time to do absolutely nothing, but have an end date for that. When I retired, I was already on the Missions Committee at church, I was on the board for a charity that was needing more of my time, and a few other things. I actually had said yes to too many things. I learned I needed to say no to some of those things. Some of these things have wound down at the same time I needed to focus on my mother's estate, so things have kinda worked themselves out."

Would you say the transition to retirement was difficult, or were you generally prepared for it?

"I was very prepared for it. I talked to other people on a "retirement panel" at work after I had been retired about a year. Everyone on the panel had supposedly retired, but some of them were still working and were having a problem trying to "wind some things up" so that they could make a clean break from their jobs. A few of the retirees were still waking up in the middle of the night, dreaming and worrying about work tasks. While I was there, my boss asked me to come back to work for one more year! I finally told her I would give her 40 hours a week for a while, but I couldn't do the 60 or 80 hour weeks any more. So I worked close to one more year, but the last 4—5 months were spent handing things off and working a pretty relaxed schedule."

What things do you now regularly enjoy doing?

"I love to travel. I have my RV and like to meet up with friends and camp. I like quilting and have set up my RV to make that possible. I like international travel too. I try to take one big trip a year. This year it's South Africa. I also still do a lot of work at church. I lead the group that goes to Guatemala, we've been going for 12 years. We take teenagers and adults down and build houses and work on church schools and churches. That takes about 3 months of my time each year."

What are some of the best things about being retired?

"Freedom. What do I want to do today? And if I do give a significant amount of time to something or feel pressured to do something, it's for something that my heart is invested in, not somebody else's agenda. Not "we gotta make this sales number" or "meet this software deadline", that kind of thing."

Anything that you don't like about retirement?

"Well. I used to worry a little bit about money, even though my financial advisor said I was okay. I had been used to if I wanted it, I bought it, because I made plenty of money. And now, well, this is kinda sad, but with the passing of my Mom, and her sister before her, I don't really have that worry anymore."

What advice would you offer for those people considering retirement?

"Have a plan. Know something you want to do in the near future, and something else you want to do a little further down the line. But it's not that I quit this job that's been messing my life up and now I have no idea what to do. Something to work towards. And a good financial advisor is always a wonderful thing."

CHAPTER 6

LET'S GET PHYSICAL

Healthy Lifestyle and Exercise

Keep moving.

It's been known for a long time that regular exercise, healthy eating, and no smoking or excessive drinking, together with the management of weight, blood pressure, and stress, will allow you to enjoy life for a longer period of time.

Don't be afraid to take medicine, if necessary, to lower blood pressure and keep LDL cholesterol in check. This is an effective and very common practice. Left untreated, high blood pressure and cholesterol leave you vulnerable to both heart attacks and strokes--including "mini-strokes" that you may not notice, but can lead to dementia.

Annual medical check-ups are also a good idea. They allow you to keep up your prescriptions while providing an opportunity for early detection of changing conditions via blood work and examinations.

Let's take a few minutes now to discuss physical exercise. I know that some of you see it as tedious and boring—maybe worse. But the evidence is clear that regular exercise helps you live better and longer; it improves both physical and mental health.

<u>Regular exercise has a positive impact on everything you do. Its intrinsic value cannot be overstated.</u>

Even routine household chores can provide a marked benefit over sitting or lying down. We all need to accept and adapt to the aging process without giving in to the lure of sloth.

Exercise can be difficult if you're not used to it. You need to do a few simple things that make it easier to engage with:

- Start Slowly
- Add Variety
- Check Results
- Make it Part of Your Routine

Some people find it easier and more enjoyable to work out with a friend, or in a class. Bottom Line: Just do it—the rewards are too high to ignore.

Try to setup a regular exercise routine with aerobic (walking, jogging, swimming, etc.), anaerobic (weightlifting, isometrics), and stretching components. Household chores, walking, and sports are all great activities, but they should be supplemented by a regular exercise routine that ensures all three of these components are addressed. Stretching is the least taxing but most overlooked of these elements. It plays an important role in staying limber and minimizing soft-tissue injuries.

If you alternate daily between aerobic and anaerobic workouts, your body will have recovery time between each type of exercise. This also keeps your routine from becoming monotonous and helps you stay motivated.

Consider exercising first thing in the morning. This will keep you from becoming distracted later by something else, it will make you feel better the rest of the day, and it eliminates the nagging burden of trying to "fit it in" to a changing daily schedule.

The following is an example of a balanced weekly exercise routine. Except for stretching, the duration times listed are for a mature routine, after some stamina has been developed. If you are just starting out, begin with 10—15 minutes of exercise and add a couple of minutes each week until you reach your desired targets. Seeing your stamina increase (measuring results) is fun and provides positive feedback:

Sunday—45 minutes of elliptical machine or boxing with a heavy punching bag

Monday—45 minutes of weightlifting, followed by 10 minutes of stretching

Tuesday—30 minutes of swimming, jogging, or any aerobic exercise machine

Wednesday—45 minutes of weightlifting, followed by 10 minutes of stretching

Thursday—30 minutes of swimming, jogging, or any aerobic exercise machine

Friday—45 minutes of weightlifting, followed by 10 minutes of stretching

Saturday—30 minutes of swimming, jogging, or any aerobic exercise machine

The aerobic activity maintains your cardiovascular stamina, keeping you from feeling out of breath during normal exertion. The weightlifting keeps your muscles and bones strong and allows you to burn more calories while resting. The stretching keeps you flexible and injury-resistant. Overall, exercise makes you look younger and feel better. It also boosts your appetite and overall energy level.

On a personal note, I enjoy a more moderate exertion in my Sunday workouts. I listen to music while I exercise in a more relaxed fashion. It gives me an enjoyable "break" and refreshing start to the day. Alternatively, you may want to give yourself a day off from exercise all-together. For many people, a day off helps them to stay energized and lets the body recover from strenuous activity. My advice would be to "listen to your body"; see how you feel and act accordingly.

Strongly consider joining a gym for at least some of these activities. The gym is a great place for social interaction, and it's easier to work hard when people around you are doing the same thing.

You can continue to exercise as you get older by adjusting technique (e.g., speed, duration, weight). This will help compensate for the effects of aging.

Finally, try to age gracefully. Don't try to compare and judge yourself physically based on what you were years ago. If you feel the need to compare and grade, make sure your comparisons are with people your own age.

W.O.W.

Exercise won't turn back the clock, but it will slow the decay.

Intimacy

In retirement, you will likely spend more time with your spouse than ever before. In the midst of this togetherness, it's important that you also give each other some space so you can both do your own thing.

Having a lifetime partner is one of life's joys, and growing old together eases the burdens of aging. Wanting to be close with someone, both emotionally and physically, is part of our DNA.

Let's talk a minute about physical intimacy.

Just like every other physical function, sexual performance degrades as we age. The wonderful thing though, is that once you accept that reality, sex can be as enjoyable as it ever was. Remember when we discussed how an exercise routine can continue as we age, by adjusting our technique? The same holds true for physical intimacy. Try to keep it going in whatever way you can. For men, don't be afraid to try sildenafil tablets (Viagra and its competitors), if and when needed, to heighten the experience. Know your body's physical tendencies and adjust conditions accordingly—practice makes perfect! For women, there are plenty of sexual aids out there that can mitigate any performance issue. And don't forget about the value of simply hugging each other. We can all benefit from simple, heartfelt human touch!

Too many couples give up on sex just because they won't adjust their "technique". The reasons can vary from embarrassment, to a faulty self-image, or maybe a lack of adventure. Often, this leads people to quit caring how they look, followed by eating more, quitting regular exercise, and "letting themselves go".

Lack of physical intimacy is a loss. People adjust to it all the time, but most wish they didn't have to.

If at all possible, don't give up on it.

W.O.W.

Avoid focusing and talking to others about your medical problems as you age. It's not good for you or the people around you.

CONCLUSION

If you're planning to retire, I hope this book helped answer some of your questions. Preparing for a change of this magnitude will help you make a smooth and enjoyable transition.

If you are planning to work as long as possible, I hope this book has provided sufficient perspective to understand thriving retirees.

In summary, the following are the fundamental components for a successful retirement:

- Funding
- Self-confidence
- Sense of Adventure; Willingness to Take Risks and Accept Failure
- Belonging to Social Group(s)--family, friends, activity, religious

We are fortunate to live in a country where many people have the opportunity for a "second life" beyond the workplace.

Whichever path you choose, here's to your continued success.

Happy Trails.

W.O.W.

The things we cared so much about at 30 are usually not

the same things we care so much about at 60. This is natural and should not be the focus of regret or scorn as we age. Try to remember your motivations throughout life and understand people of all ages. This will help you avoid blanket condemnations of younger generations.

APPENDIX

Top 25 Retirement Locations in the U.S. (2019 US News and World Report)

Derived from 125 largest metropolitan areas in the country with consideration given to housing affordability, happiness, desirability, retiree taxes, job market, and health care. The list is weighted based on a survey of people 45 years of age and older regarding their retirement preferences.

1—Fort Meyers, Florida

2—Sarasota, Florida

3--Lancaster, Pennsylvania

4—Asheville, North Carolina

5--Port St. Lucie, Florida

6—Jacksonville, Florida

7—Winston-Salem, North Carolina

8—Nashville, Tennessee

9—Grand Rapids, Michigan

10—Dallas-Ft. Worth, Texas

11—Austin, Texas

12—Manchester, New Hampshire

13—Knoxville, Tennessee

14—Miami, Florida

15—Lakeland, Florida

16—Fort Wayne, Indiana

17—Tampa, Florida

18—Pittsburgh, Pennsylvania

19—Melbourne, Florida

20--Portland, Oregon

21—Chattanooga, Tennessee

22—Orlando, Florida

23—Allentown, Pennsylvania

24—El Paso, Texas

25—Harrisburg, Pennsylvania

For more information go to:

https://money.usnews.com/money/retirement/
slideshows/the-best-places-to-retire?onepage

Top 5 Financial Companies for Individual Investors
(Investopedia, 2019)

1—The Vanguard Group

2—Pacific Investment Management Company, LLC

3—BlackRock, Inc.

4—Fidelity Investments

5—Invesco Ltd.

For more information, go to:

https://www.investopedia.com/articles/
investing/022316/top-5-asset-management-firms-
portfolios-2016-pimco-blk.asp

Top 7 Financial Magazines (investorjunkie 2019)

1—Barron's

2—The Economist

3—Kiplinger's

4—Investor's Business Daily

5—Bloomberg Business Week

6—Forbes

7—Money

For more information, go to:

https://investorjunkie.com/investing/top-financial-magazines/

20 Tips for Making Retirement Travel Fulfilling (NewRetirement 2019)

1—Set Goals, Make a Bucket List, Think Through Where You Want to Go--With Whom? Why?

2—Are You and Your Spouse in Agreement?

3—Don't Stick to the Tried and True Destinations

4—Did You Know That Seniors Get Discounts on Hotels and Airfare?

5—Forgo Hotels Altogether

6—Have You Considered Renting Out Your Own Home to Fund Retirement Travel?

7—Resources For Last Minute Retirement Travel

8—Take Time to Plan—Scientists Say it is the Best Part

9—Plan Longer Trips and Save

10—How About a Really Long Trip: Have You Considered Life on the Road?

11—No Matter the Length of Your Road Trip—Here Are Some Great Resources

12—Resources for Discounted Trips

For more information, go to:

 https://www.newretirement.com/retirement/20-retirement-travel-ideas/

ABOUT THE AUTHOR

After a 30 year career in engineering and management, Les Hoffman retired in 2008 at the age of 51. In addition to *RETIRE?*, he has written two novels, *Sudden Justice* and *Border Justice*. He is an amateur actor and boxer and lives with his wife and three dogs in Pell City, Alabama. (www.facebook.com/leshoffmanjustice)